MEL BAY'S GUITAR DAILY PRACTICE HANDBOOK

by
William Bay

MW00652709

BOOK CONTENTS

CD CONTENTS

1	Tuning [2:37]	25	Key of Dm [:44]	49	Study #4 [:26]	73	Key of A [:19]
2	#1 Part 2 (pg. 3) [:45]	26	Key of Bb (pg. 12) [:36]	50	Study #5 [:26]	74	Key of F#m [:20]
3	#2 Part 1 [:45]	27	Key of Gm [:44]	51	Study #6 [:24]	75	Key of D [:18]
4	#2 Part 2 [:46]	28	Key of Eb [:44]	52	Study #7 [:25]	76	Key of Bm [:18]
5	#3 Part 1 [:45]	29	Key of Cm [:46]	53	Study #8 [:25]	77	Key of G [:21]
6	#3 Part 2 [:45]	30	Key of Ab (pg. 13) [:46]	54	Study #9 [:43]	78	Key of Em [:34]
7	#4 [1:06]	31	Key of Fm [:45]	55	Arpeggio Study, Key of C [:38]	79	Harmonized Scales, C-Cm [2:52]
8	#5 [1:06]	32	Key of Db/C# [:47]	56	Key of Am [:19]	80	Ab-C#m [3:21]
9	#1 (pg. 4) [:20]	33	Key of Bbm [:45]	57	Key of F [:18]	81	A-Dm [2:01]
10	#2 [:22]	34	Key of Gb/F# [:40]	58	Key of Dm [:20]	82	Thirds, C-Dm [1:37]
11	#3 [:21]	35	Key of Ebm [:45]	59	Key of Bb [:20]	83	Bb-Ebm [3:23]
12	#4 [:20]	36	Key of B [:37]	60	Key of Gm [:19]	84	B-Em [3:31]
13	#5 [:21]	37	Key of G#m [:46]	61	Key of Eb [:20]	85	Position Studies/ Sight Reading [2:18]
14	Picking Etude #1 [:33]	38	Key of E (pg. 15) [:45]	62	Key of Cm [:17]	86	2nd Position [:43]
15	Picking Etude #2 [:33]	39	Key of C#m [:46]	63	Key of Ab [:21]	87	3rd Position [:26]
16	Barcelona [:37]	40	Key of A [:45]	64	Key of Fm [:20]	88	4th Position [:24]
17	Song (pg. 7) [:38]	41	Key of F#m [:47]	65	Key of Db/C# [:21]	89	5th Position [:29]
18	11 Mile Canyon [1:00]	42	Key of D (pg. 16) [:45]	66	Key of Bbm [:19]	90	6th Position [:27]
19	Boston Bay [1:19]	43	Key of Bm [:45]	67	Key of Gb/F# [:22]	91	7th Position [:25]
20	Timberline Reel [:49]	44	Key of G [:47]	68	Key of Ebm [:18]	92	8th Position [:27]
21	Scale Studies [:22]	45	Key of Em [:46]	69	Key of B [:18]	93	9th Position [:24]
22	Key of C [:41]	46	Left Hand Study #1 [:51]	70	Key of G#m [:21]	94	Conclusion [:25]
23	Key of Am [:44]	47	Study #2 [:24]	71	Key of E [:20]		
24	Key of F [:44]	48	Study #3 [:27]	72	Key of C#m [:17]		

Visit us on the Web at http://www.melbay.com — E-mail us at email@melbay.com

MEL BAY ®

Right Hand Picking Technique

Preparatory Picking Studies

[Play all studies with ⊓ V alternate picking]

Fingerstyle = im-im or ma-ma

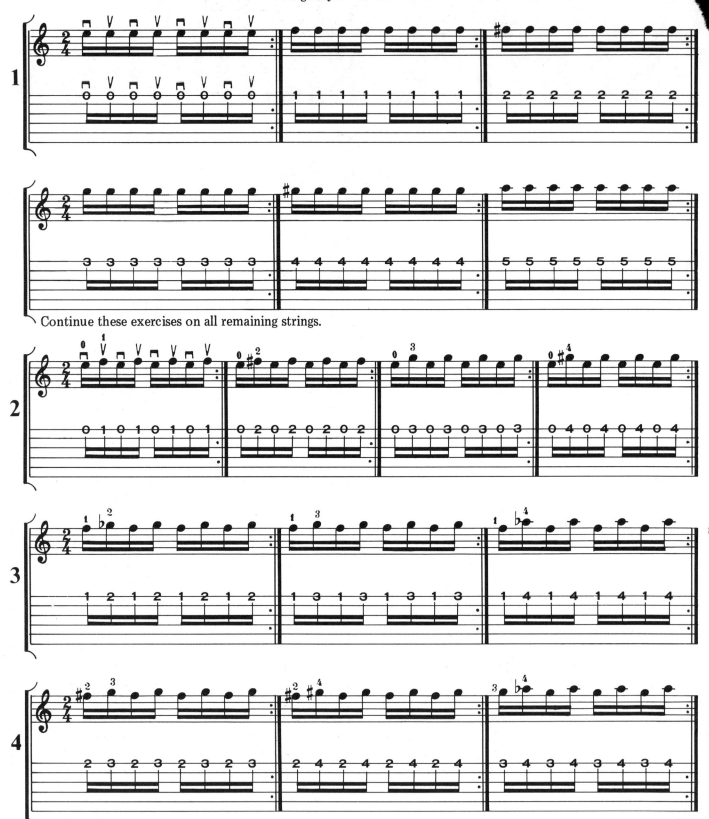

Continue these exercises on all remaining strings.

Continue these exercises on all remaining strings.

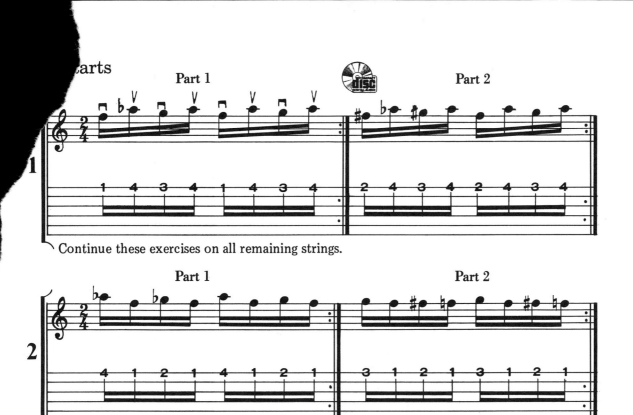

Continue these exercises on all remaining strings.

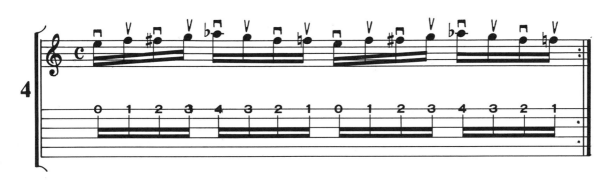

Continue this exercise on all remaining strings.

Continue these exercises on all remaining strings.

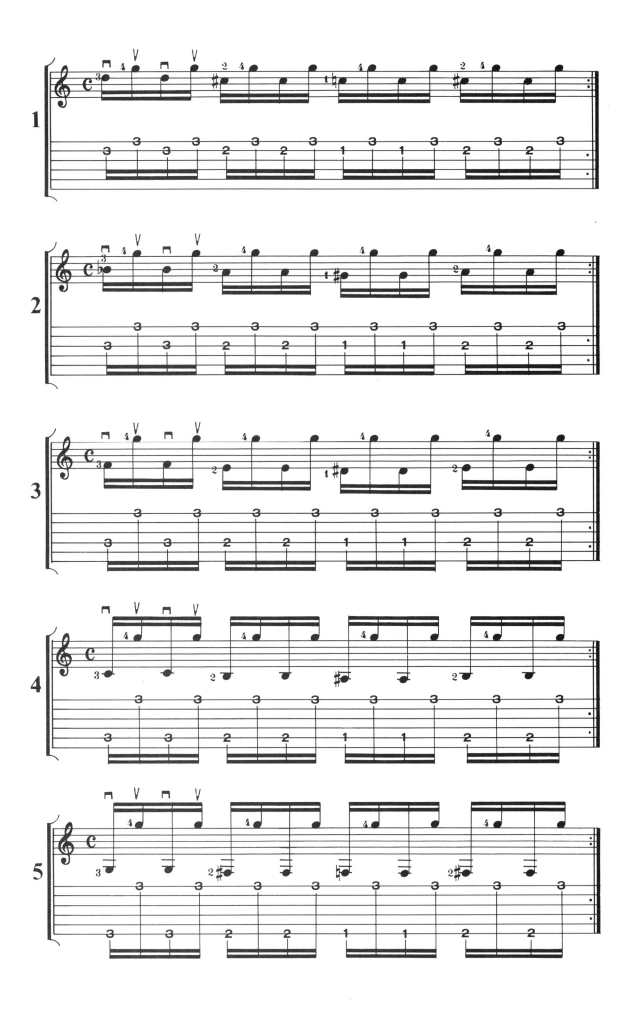

Picking Etude #1

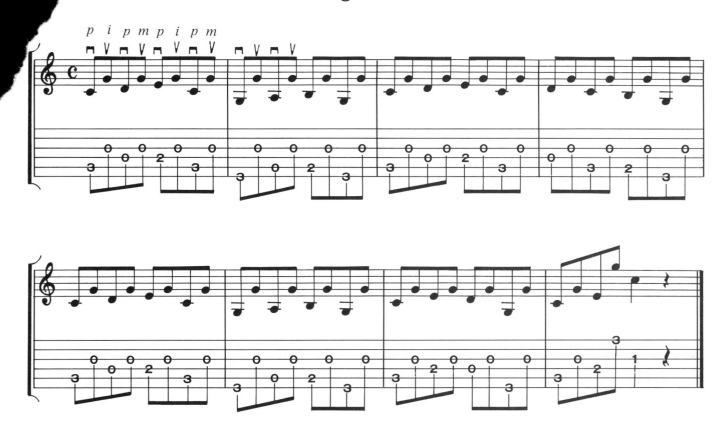

Picking Etude #2

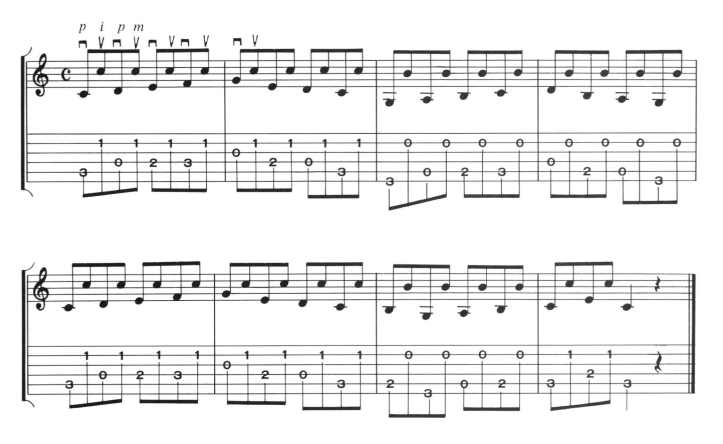

Barcelona

William

Song

William Bay

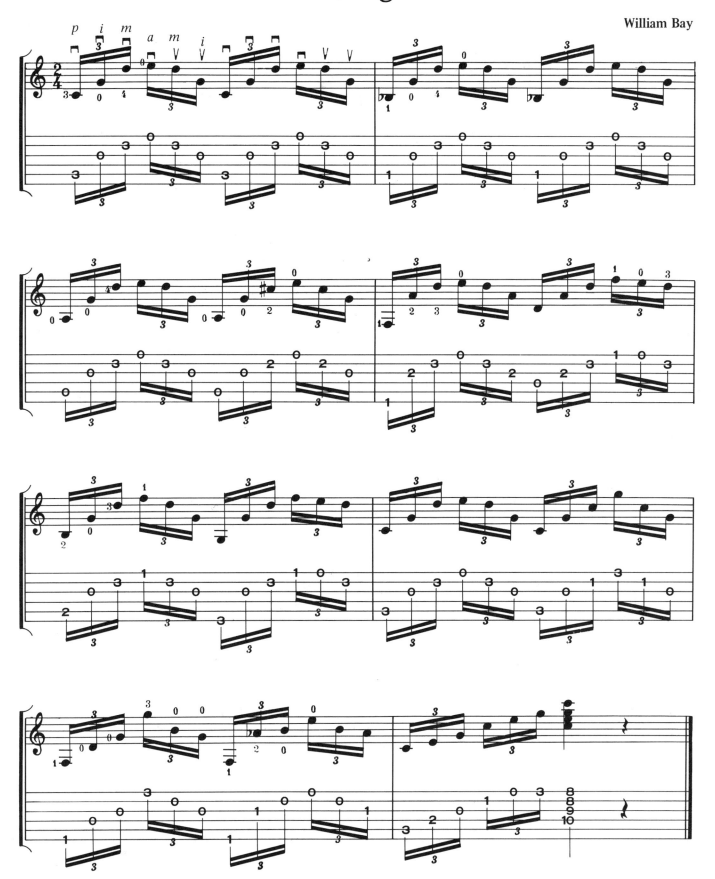

11 Mile Canyon

William Bay

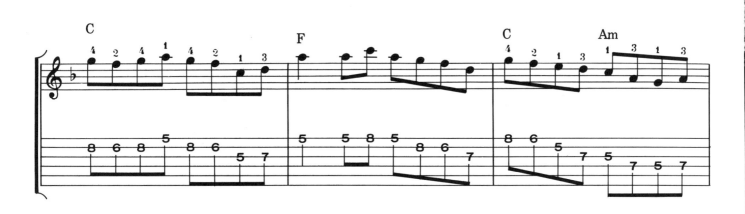

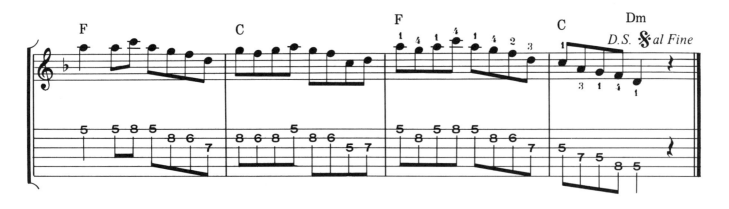

Solos Based On Scale Steps
BOSTON BAY

Traditional

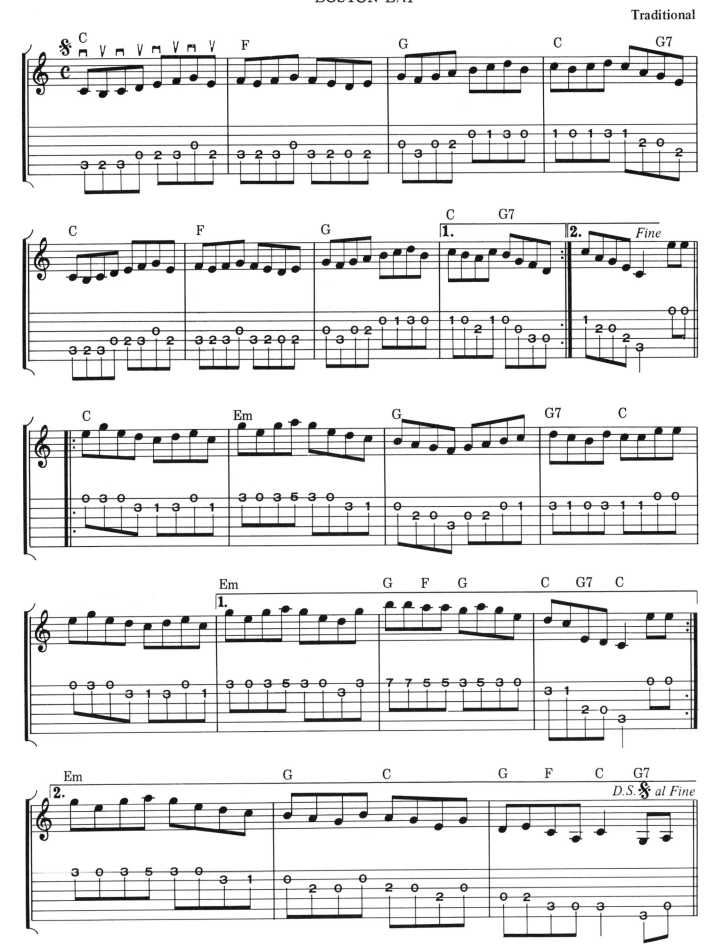

9

Timberline Reel

William Bay

Scale Studies

Scale Workout (Practice all scales ascending and descending.   Alternate pick ⊓ ∨ each scale)

C

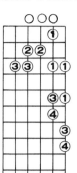  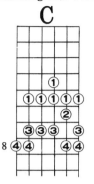 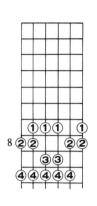 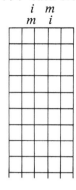

Am

  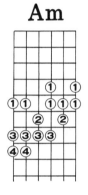 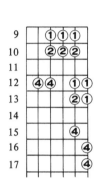 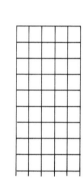

F

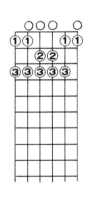 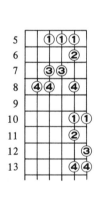  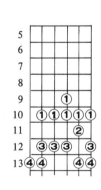 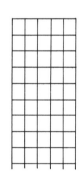

Dm

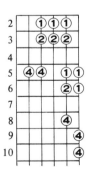 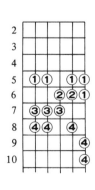 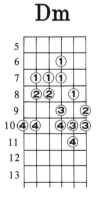 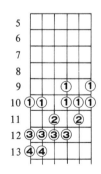 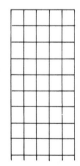

B♭

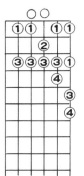 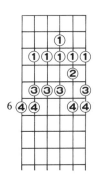 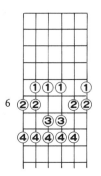 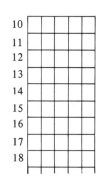 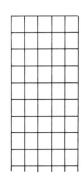

Gm

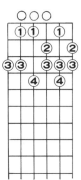 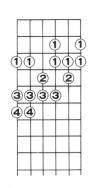 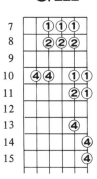 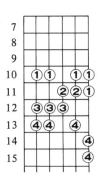 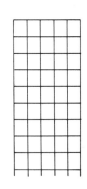

E♭

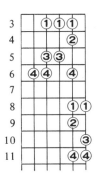 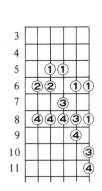 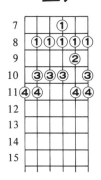 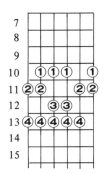 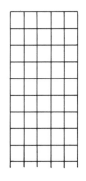

Cm

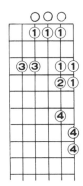 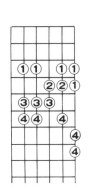 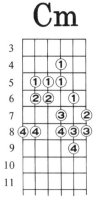 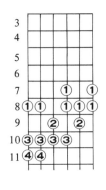

A♭

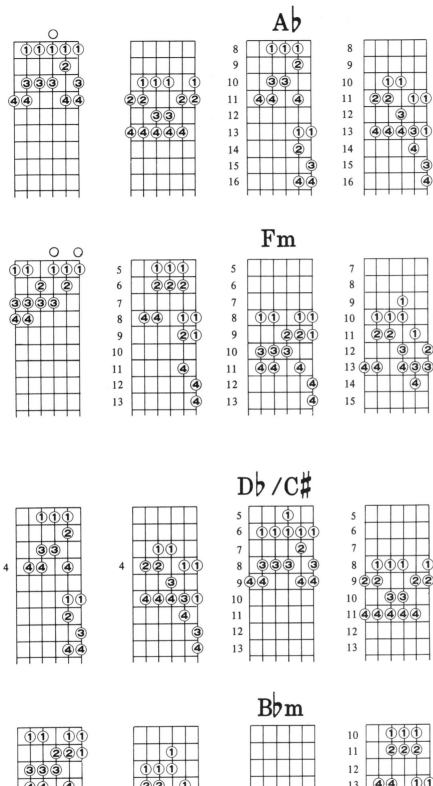

Fm

D♭/C♯

B♭m

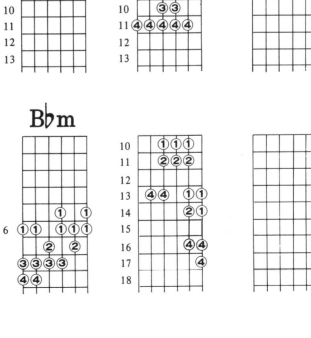

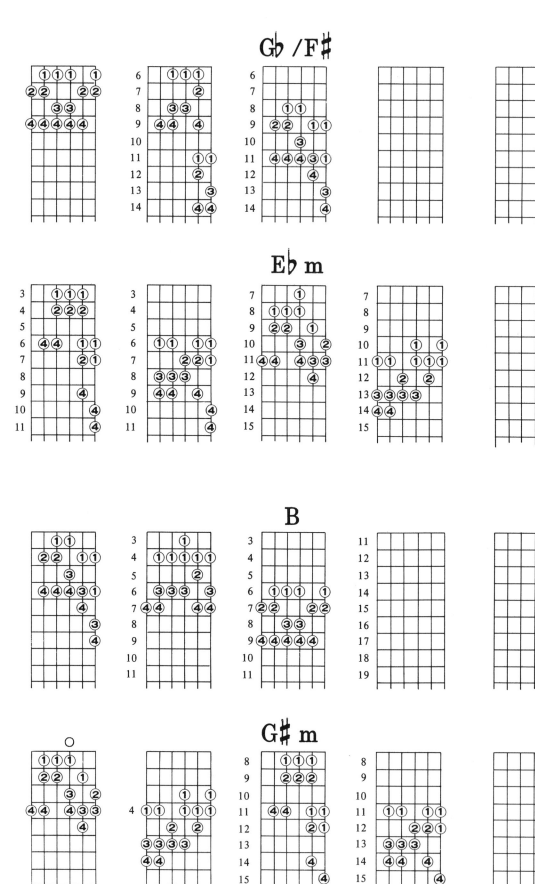

14

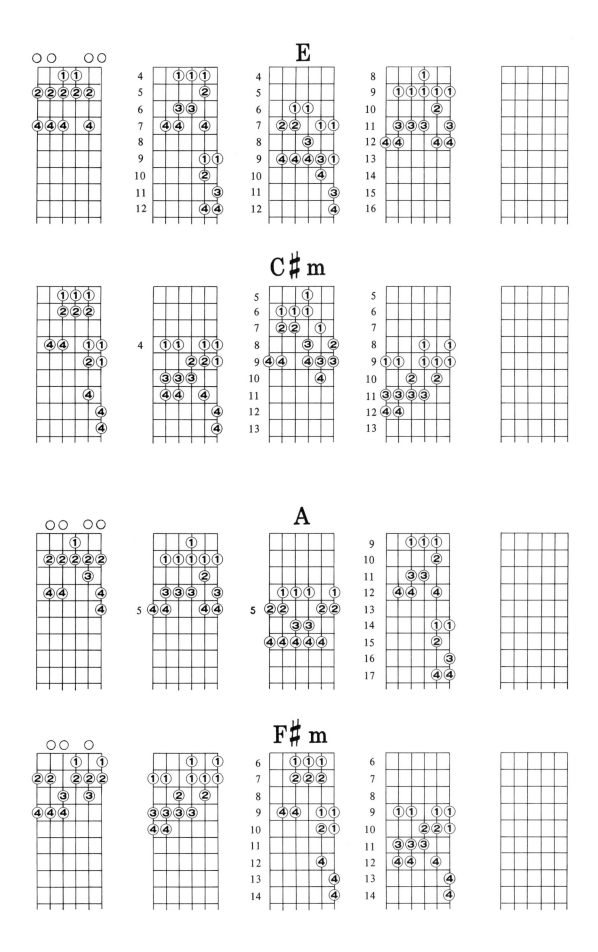

15

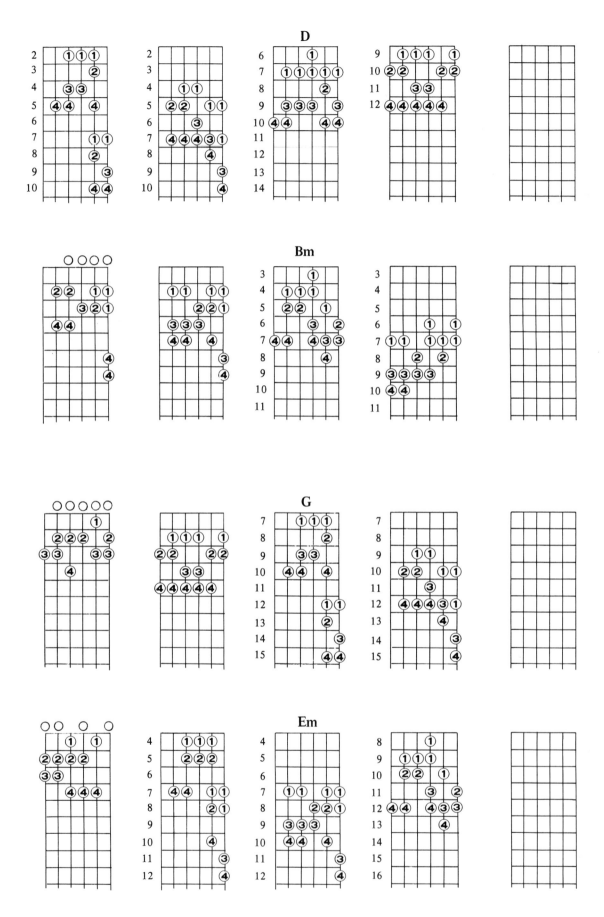

Left Hand Studies

Strive for ease of movement and clear sound

Study #1–Downward Movement

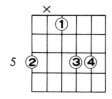 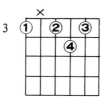 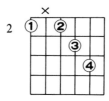 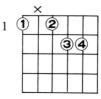

Continue up Chromatically

Study #2–Stretching Study

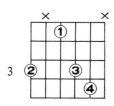 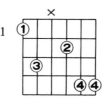

Continue up Chromatically

Study #3–Thumb Study

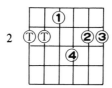

Continue up Chromatically

Study #4–Inside/Outside

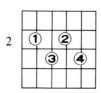 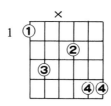

Continue up Chromatically

17

Study #5-Major 6/7

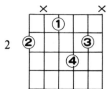 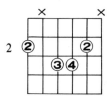

Continue up Chromatically

Study #6-Outside Voicing

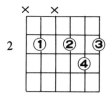

Continue up Chromatically

Study #7-Inside Stretch

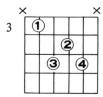 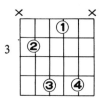

Continue up Chromatically

Study #8-Open/Closed Hand

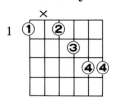 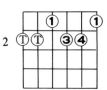

Continue up Chromatically

Study #9-Descending Thumb

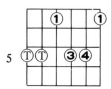 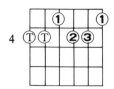 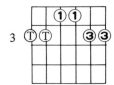

Continue up Chromatically

18

Arpeggio Studies

These studies have the effect of making the Guitar fingerboard feel "Shorter." They will make movement up the neck easier.

Arpeggios (Use alternate picking) Play ascending and descending.

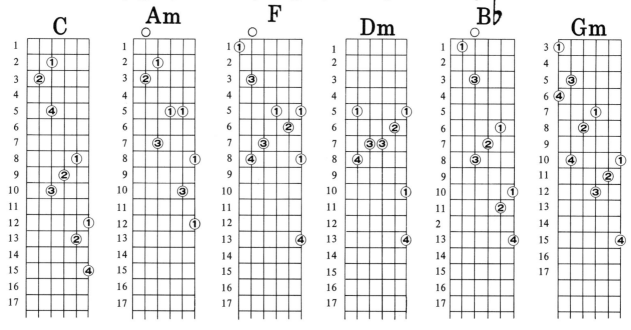

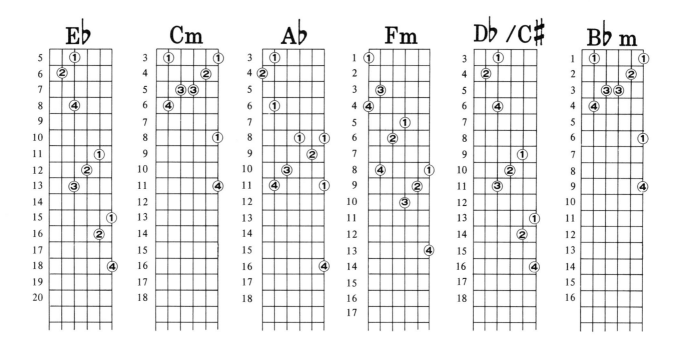

19

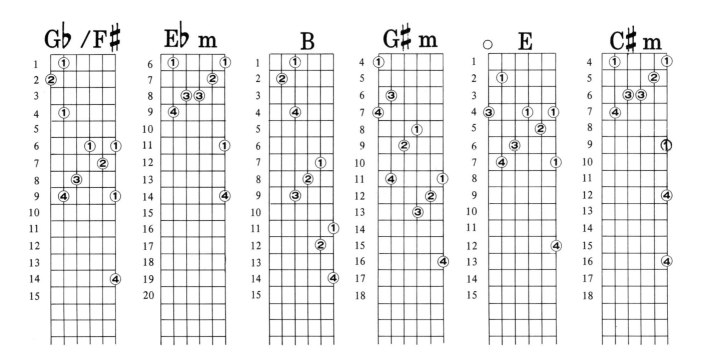

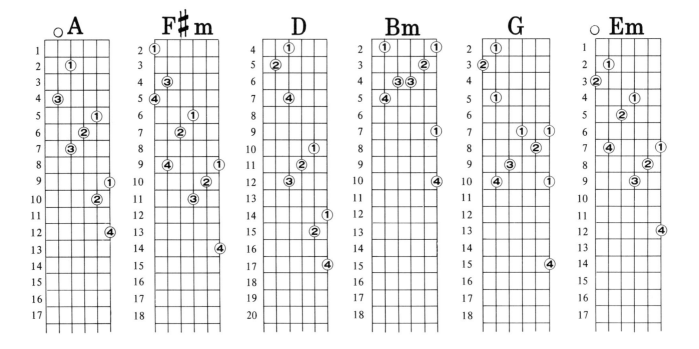

20

Harmonized Scales

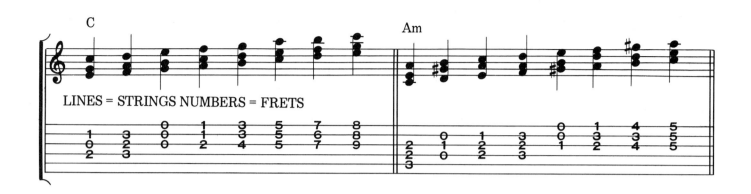

LINES = STRINGS NUMBERS = FRETS

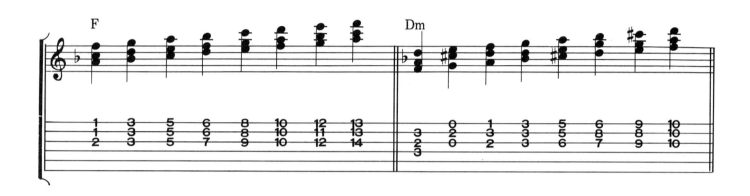

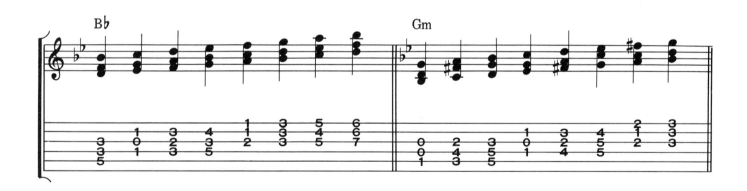

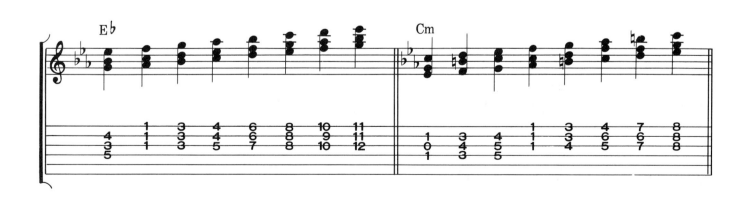

21

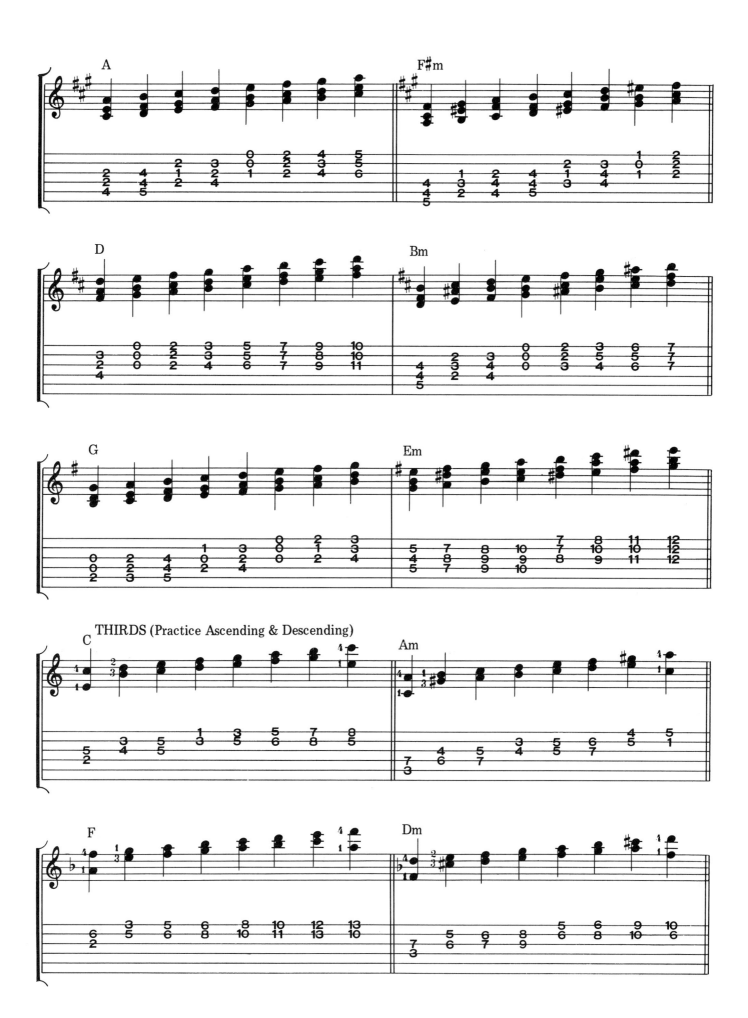

THIRDS (Practice Ascending & Descending)

23

24

Position Studies/Sight Reading Development

1st Position

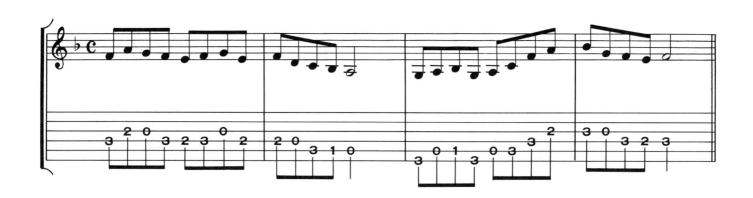

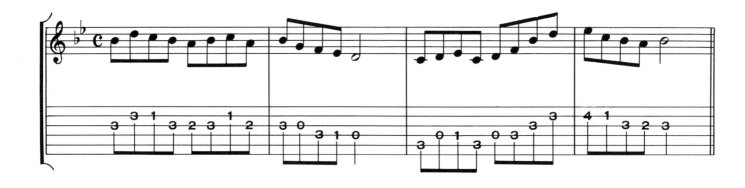

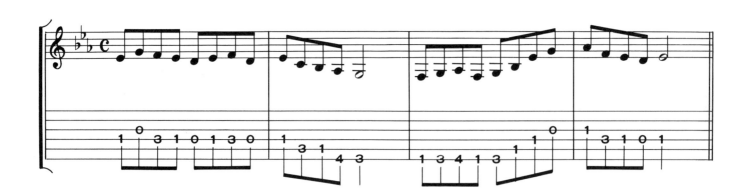

26

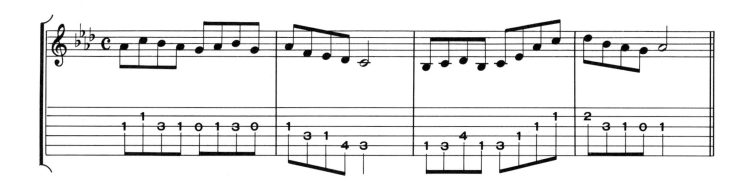

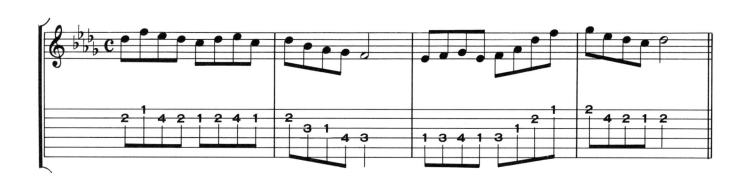

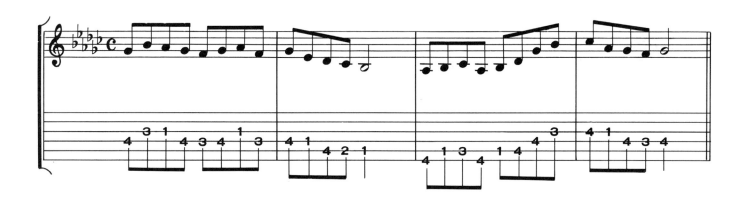

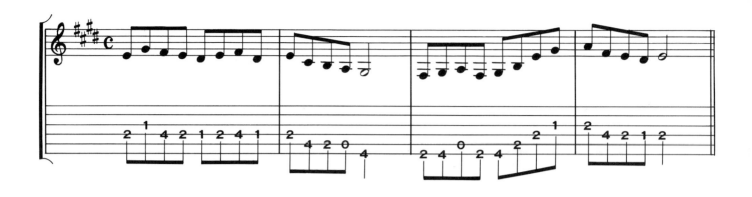

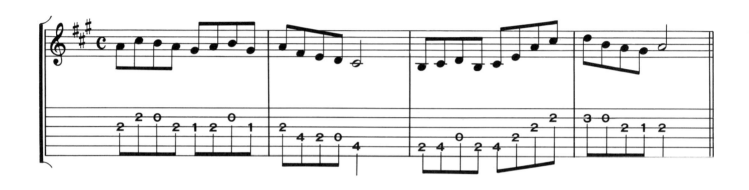

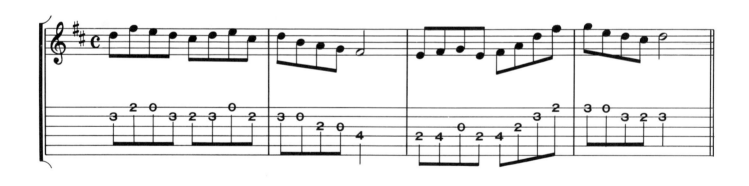

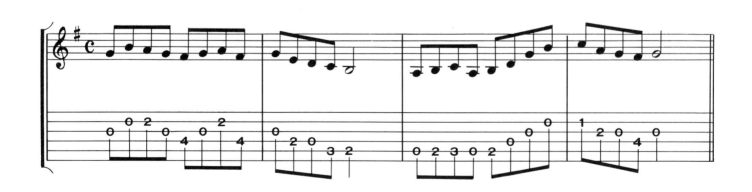

2nd Position

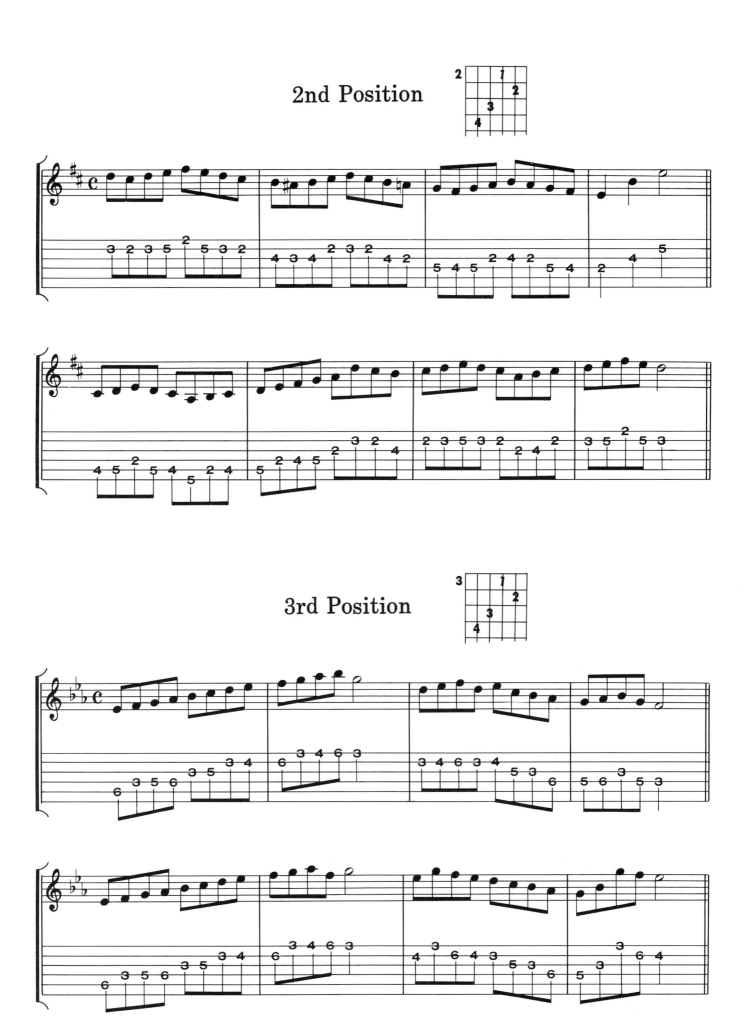

3rd Position

4th Position

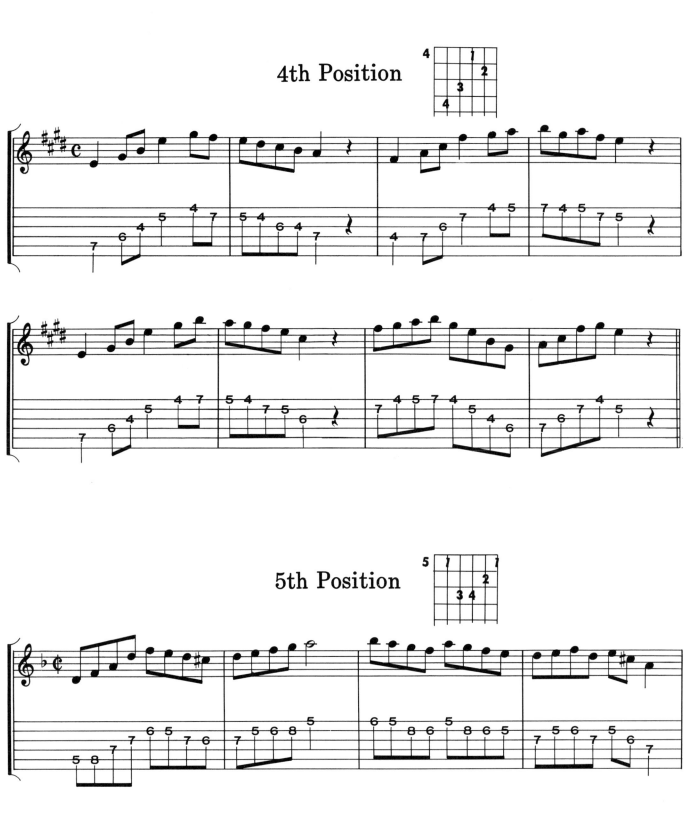

5th Position

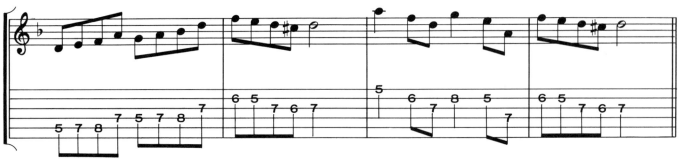

6th Position

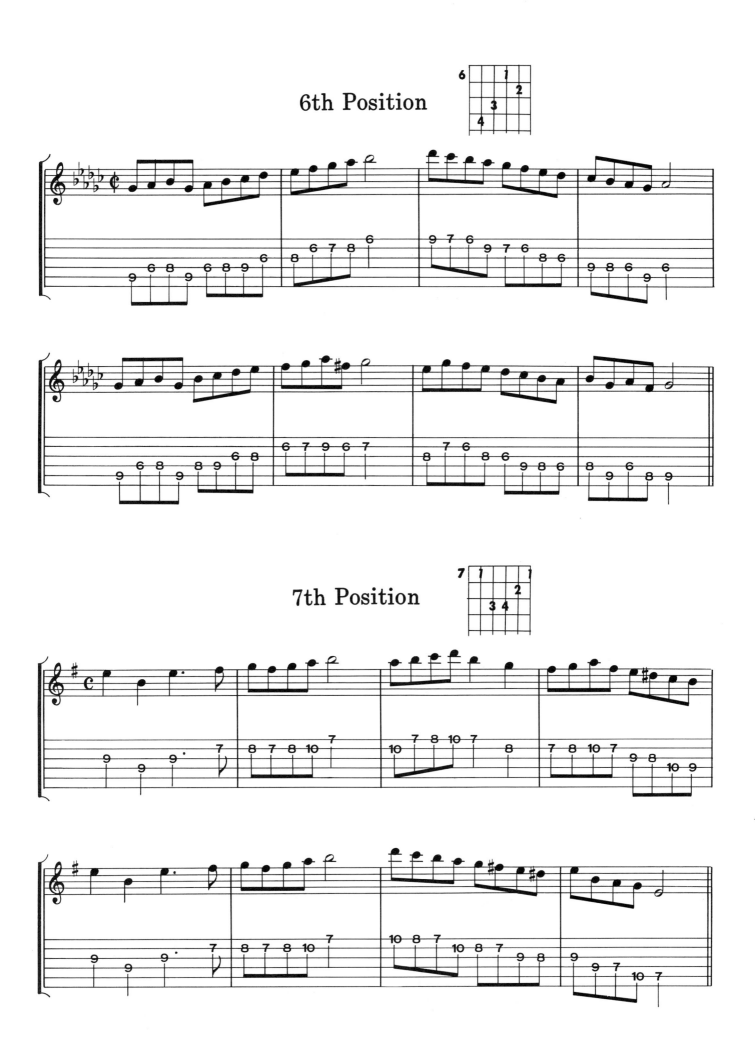

7th Position

8th Position

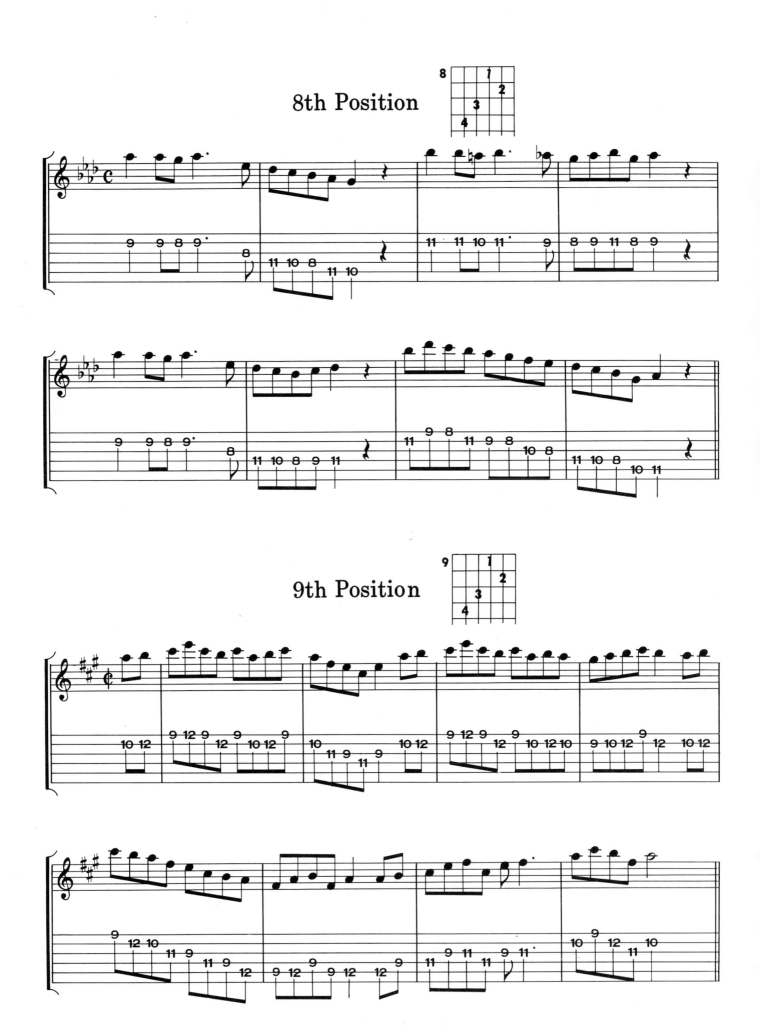

9th Position

32